Anatomy of a Castle: The Weobley Castle Project

edited by
George Nash & George Children

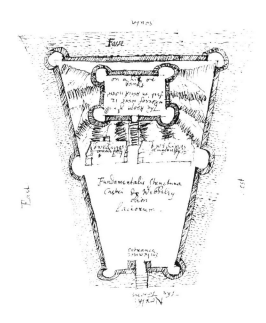

Logaston Press

LOGASTON PRESS
Little Logaston Woonton Almeley
Herefordshire HR3 6QH

THE WEOBLEY CASTLE PROJECT
Weobley & District History Society

Published by Logaston Press 2003
in association with
Weobley & District History Society

Copyright text © Weobley & District History Society 2003

ISBN 1 904396 11 9

Set in Times by Logaston Press
and printed in Great Britain by
The Cromwell Press

Contents

Foreword

My interest in the castle began over 30 years ago, following a series of lectures on Weobley by Muriel Tonkin. However, I visited the castle 40 years previously as a boy. Since then I have always had a keen interest in local history. As well as the castle, I was interested in the nearby Garnstone Estate and for many years researched its history. With the castle in mind, and retirement pending, I managed to persuade the History Society to think about a possible long-term project that would benefit the Society and the community of Weobley. The castle, which, in my view, had a very fragmentary history, appeared to be a likely candidate, so, in 1998, I managed to talk to a local archaeologist about a possible project that would not only involve the castle but also its surroundings. I was interested in understanding the relationship between the medieval history of the castle and the post-medieval history of Garnstone Estate. I thought that a project involving a number of scientific disciplines would enable us to further understand the landscape surrounding the castle. The Weobley and District History Society, of which I am a founder member, took on this idea wholeheartedly and set in motion preparations for a landscape project. The fieldwork that was undertaken in 2002 formed only part of a long-term project; I hope to see excavation based on the results of the 2002 season. I would finally mention that this project is unique in bringing together professional field-workers and the community to create what I would term 'living history'.

Bill Dyer
August 2003

Preface

This project was funded by the Local Heritage Initiative and undertaken by teaching staff from the Centre for the Historic Environment, Department of Archaeology University of Bristol with documentary research by Valerie Goodbury. Further work within the scope of the project was undertaken by David Lovelace, Duncan James, Mike Smith and Jim Tonkin. The team were assisted by members of the Weobley & District History Society and volunteers from the village. This first phase of the project ran between August and December 2002. Additional research, in the form of a Ground Penetrating Radar (GPR) survey and cartographic digitisation, were undertaken by specialists and staff from University College London and the University of Cambridge.

Many castle sites are Scheduled Ancient Monuments (SAMs) and Weobley Castle is no exception. Little thought has generally been given to the area immediately beyond the limits of the scheduled area, suggesting that the castle was a self-contained unit and that the economic, political and social infrastructure was contained within its walls. This is not the case. The principal aim of the project was to look beyond the castle, in particular at earthworks on the northern, southern and western flanks of the inner bailey. The results of the investigations show that the castle depended on the surrounding catchment for its survival. More importantly, the project was able to outline the castle's history and reveal a much earlier landscape immediately to the west.

The editors of this volume would like to thank the following bodies and individuals. Firstly, the Local Heritage Initiative, which provided much of the funding. Thanks also to Mr. James Verdin, landowner, who very kindly granted permission for the archaeologists and members of the local community to record every hump and bump on his land; and to the householders who live within the line of the outer bailey of the castle. We are also grateful to Andy Johnson of Logaston Press for logistical help, timetabling and advice on the production of the book; to Sue Hubbard of Herefordshire Records Office and Simon Neal of The British Library; to Dr. Kate Harris, Librarian at Longleat; to botanists Peter and Stephanie Thompson and Barbara Redwood; and to Rebecca Roseff and Melissa Seddon of Herefordshire Sites and Monuments Record. Finally, sincere thanks for the support of members of the Weobley & District History Society and volunteers, in particular committee members Brian Redwood, Gina Harley, Norman Haynes, Roy Maunder, Jim Tonkin, Walter Fletcher and photographers Tony Morris, Donald Kilgour and Barbara Redwood. Without your efforts, come rain or shine, the project would never have taken off.

Setting the Scene

In 2000, members of Weobley & District History Society got together to form a committee with one simple aim: to find out as much as possible about a ruinous tump, the remains of a once powerful castle that stood at the southern end of the village (Map 1).

It was known that a castle was built by the de Lacy family sometime in the 12th century, that it played a role during the turbulent times of Stephen and Matilda and that it was rebuilt on a grander scale sometime after 1216. Throughout the Middle Ages, records show that the castle and borough of

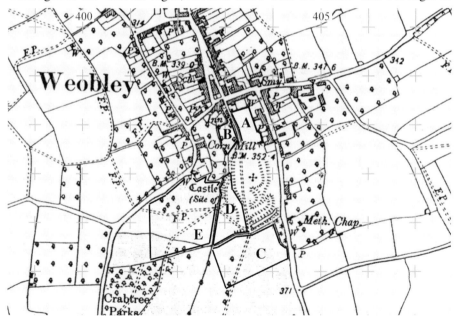

Map 1. Plan of the castle earthworks on the Ordnance Survey map of 1887, also showing the areas A-E referred to in the text

Weobley developed hand in hand. However, for reasons that are not entirely clear, the 16th century saw the castle sidelined. No longer a thriving social and economic centre, it gradually sank into obscurity. By the 17th century it was little more than a memory.

Now, thanks to sophisticated survey techniques (including the use of ground penetrating radar and magnetic survey equipment), diligent scholarship and the enthusiastic involvement of local people, the life of the castle is being reconstructed piece by piece. A series of features and structures, including ponds, an associated leat and pond system and a possible mill, have been revealed; and evidence of pre-castle activity to the west of the castle suggests Weobley has origins reaching back to the Iron Age, if not earlier. As to the fate of the castle buildings, a team of standing building specialists have been studying houses adjoining the castle grounds in an attempt to locate any re-used masonry.

With a wealth of new information, and backed by funding from the Local Heritage initiative, the Weobley Castle Project is now looking forward to the possibility of carrying out further investigations, including excavation of the castle mound itself.

This book details the findings so far and looks ahead to unearthing more secrets that have lain buried for 400 years.

1 WHAT OF THE EVIDENCE?

The castle that antiquarian John Leland visited around 1535 had passed from glory to ruin. Weobley, he says, 'is a market towne in Herfordeshire, where is a goodly castell, but somewhat in decay'. Probably constructed shortly after 1216 as a visual statement of wealth and power, the impressive building soon suffered the neglect of an absent owner, a pattern that was to continue throughout its entire existence. The last official reference found to the 'castle and manor' is in 1508. Soon after that, as Leland tells us, its condition was poor. Less than a century later, it appears, the castle was no more. A lease of 1614 includes 'the site of the castle of Weobley'. Apart from the mill, no buildings are mentioned. The walls of the castle, once 'good and strong', had evidently all but vanished, the remains no doubt providing a useful source of building stone for use elsewhere in the village. This chapter traces the story of the castle from its construction to its demise using existing archaeological and historical information.

The castle remains, according to the Royal Commission on Historical Monuments (England) (RCHME), comprise a double-ditched earthwork and oval bailey.[1] The (inner) bailey measures approximately 77m x 66m, with a series of large ramparts located on the eastern side of the earthwork, and is surrounded by a moat of which only remnants survive on the eastern and southern flanks (Plate 1). These remains lie to the south of Weobley, one of Herefordshire's 29 medieval towns. Weobley parish occupies gently undulating fertile terrain drained by the Stretford Brook which joins the River Arrow 8km north-east at Ivington Court. A small hillock known as Windmill Knapp rises 40m above the plain a few hundred metres west of the present village and where there is evidence of a mill from the 13th century. The south

---

1. The Royal Commission on Historical Monuments England (RCHME) has now been absorbed into English Heritage

*Plate 1. Survival of the moat, located on the southern flank
of the earthworks (photo: G.H. Nash)*

of the parish rises 200m up the limestone capped, wooded Burton and Wormesley hills, prominent landscape features visible for many miles.

Although the village has received much scholarly attention (RCHM 1934, Pevsner 1962, Salt 1953 and Tonkin 1971), there are a number of gaps in the historical record, in particular concerning the demise of the castle and the development of the town during the late Medieval and early post-Medieval period. The surveys undertaken in 2002 have provided much useful information on the development of the castle and have shown that people were utilising the surrounding landscape during the Iron Age, if not earlier.

Prehistory: peopling the landscape

Prehistoric settlement in this part of Herefordshire can be traced as far back as the Iron Age. The large hill enclosures of Credenhill (SO 450 446), located north-west of Hereford and some 8km south of Weobley, and Ivington Camp (SO 485 546), located south-west of Leominster and 6km east Weobley, suggest the existence of tribal groups at that time. Covering some 20ha, the sheer size of Credenhill suggests that its sphere of influence was considerable and may have encompassed the Weobley area, although any such inference must be viewed with caution; the extent of tribal territories at this time can not be established with any accuracy.

The evidence is rather fragmentary for earlier periods. Several Middle Palaeolithic Acheulian (*c.*200,000 BC) hand axes have been found in fields around Sarnesfield. However, it is more than probable that these are the result of (recent) secondary deposition. There is also evidence for human activity during the Neolithic period (4,000 BC - 2,000BC). A Neolithic axe was found at Throne Farm and another within the village. The Throne Farm axe (SO 4000 5300) is made from polished flint. The second example (SO 4000 5100) deserves further comment. According to the Herefordshire Sites and Monuments Record, this polished stone axe comes from the Graig Lwyd axe factory at Penmaenmawr, in North Wales, indicating that it had travelled over a considerable distance, probably through a process of contact and exchange between early farming groups. The owner would no doubt have gained considerable prestige from acquiring such an object (Children & Nash 1994).

Evidence for Bronze Age activity is, again, fragmentary. In 1999, a field-walking project located a small flint assemblage at Fenhampton (SO 3915 5032); and, representing an interesting Bronze Age phenomenon, a cup-marked stone has been discovered lying against a farmhouse at Lower Newton (SO 4000 5340). Cup-marks are small indentations carved into stone surfaces and possibly represent some form of 'signature' identifying land ownership. The Lower Newton example has five small cup-marks and a diagonal line and was incorporated into a series of steps used as a horse mount.

In addition to these discoveries, many findspots awaiting inclusion within the Sites and Monuments Record inventory suggest that later prehistoric activity within the area was intense. A small number of sites have been discovered as a result of responsible metal detecting, their location having been logged with the village museum.

Roman and Romano-British Evidence

Field-name evidence in the west of the parish (Richardson, 1996:458) and a small number of coins and some metalwork found in and around the village suggest significant Roman activity, possibly close to the castle. Finds listed in the Herefordshire Sites and Monuments Record include a denarius of Vespasian (found by Dr. J.H. Perrot), a coin of unknown denomination dating to the time of Constantine the Great and another from the reign of Victorinus, which was found by Major A.E.W. Salt in 1949. Metal detecting has revealed further finds, especially in fields west of the castle and east and north of The Ley. These include three Roman coins (Windmill Knap), a fibula (Horse Pastures), a sestertius (a field immediately west of Windmill Knap) and a denarius and half denarius (a field east of Weobley church).

Saxon Evidence

Early Germanic settlers often extended and renamed existing Romano-British farmland (Sherlock & Pikes 2001). Evidence of activity in and around Weobley during this period is extremely tenuous.

Domesday Book lists a number of settlements that were in existence before the Norman invasion. These include Dilwyn, Fernhill, Norton Canon, Sarnesfield, Wormsley and, of course, Weobley. The place-name Weobley is recorded as *Wibelai*, meaning 'Wibba's clearing', the latter element suggesting 'a permanent glade or clearing in woodland' (Coplestone-Crow, 1989). There seems to be no problem with the generally accepted derivation of Wibba, as a personal name, and ley, the clearing made by him or his people in order to create a settlement. Salt (1953:5) follows Canon Bannister in suggesting a possible identification with a Wibba, son of Crida, perhaps the first king of Mercia, in the late 6th century. Domesday records the first known lord of Weobley, pre-conquest, as Edwin, 'Edwi cilt' (young nobleman) (Thorn, 1983:10,48). A priest is mentioned suggesting that a church was built before the conquest. A pre-Conquest fortification is also possible, although Domesday does not mention a castle at Weobley.

Medieval Weobley and the Castle

After the Conquest, Weobley passed to William fitz Osbern, Earl of Hereford, who established by-laws designed to develop trade by encouraging immigration from Normandy. A rebellion by Fitz Osbern's heir, Roger of Breteuil, was thwarted in 1074 by Walter de Lacy, who became a tenant-in-chief of the crown after Roger forfeited his lands (Hillaby, 1985). Walter fell to his death from St. Peter's Church, in Hereford, during its construction in 1085 and his lands passed to his son, Roger, who held Weobley at the time of the Domesday survey in 1086. Weobley was the head (caput) of the de Lacy honour and a castle was probably built by Roger or his brother Hugh (Dalwood 1996; Salt 1953; Shoesmith 1996; Tonkin 1971 & Ray 2001).

The castle was garrisoned on behalf of the Empress Matilda against Stephen in 1139. Steven besieged and captured the castle from Geoffrey

Talbot the following year (Phillot 1888). The first official mention of the castle appears in the pipe rolls of 1186/7 and 1187/8, when it was in the hands of Henry II. At this time, the interests of the de Lacy family lay overseas in Ireland. Weobley only achieved political significance during the turbulent times of the second Walter de Lacy, who married Margaret, daughter of William de Braose, lord of Brecon. De Braose used the castle in his rebellion against King John in 1208 and it was whilst at Weobley, according to tradition, that he received the king's demand that he should surrender and give his son as hostage. Another tradition is that it was from Weobley Castle that de Braose set out to burn Leominster (Hillaby 1985:207).

As a result of his association with the revolt, Walter de Lacy's lands were confiscated. He regained them with some difficulty in 1213 and is likely to have proclaimed his position by building an impressive new castle at Weobley, probably concurrent with major work on his castles in Ireland and possibly at Longtown (Hillaby 1985). In the absence of documentary evidence, and subject to archaeological investigation, sometime shortly after 1216 would seem to be the most likely date for the construction of Weobley's latest and most substantial castle. Throughout this period Walter extended his power and influence in the City of Hereford and throughout the March. He was granted the custody of Hereford Castle in 1216 (Hillaby 1985:208). From 1216-1223 he was Sheriff of the county (Duncumb 1804). It was in his position as Sheriff that he was responsible for implementing the new royal policy of peace towards and protection of the Jews.

The foundation of the borough of Weobley appears to date to the mid-13th century. A fair was held before 1231—as it was in that year that Walter de Lacy petitioned for a change of date—and Weobley is represented in 1255 by its own jury at the court of eyre, presided over by the king's justices. This is seen as confirming its status as a borough at that date (Beresford 1973:124). Whereas some boroughs, such as Ludlow, were deliberately planned in the medieval period, the settlement of Weobley developed more organically. The street plans of the two boroughs illustrate the difference (Noble, 1964:65). It is possible that Walter de Lacy, having built his impressive and expensive new castle c.1216, saw the creation of burgages, or the expansion of their number, as a way of recouping some of his expenditure.

From 1295 to 1303 Weobley sent members to Parliament, and evidence for this status as a parliamentary borough was accepted as evidence for its re-enfranchisement in 1628. Proof positive that it was a borough by 1229 is given in a dispute between Nicholaus Parvus and Gilbert de Lacy (and others), as recorded in the Patent Rolls of 1225-32,[2] regarding some land and a burgage in Weobley.

When Walter died in 1241 both the Herefordshire line of the de Lacy family and the honour of Weobley came to an end. His granddaughter Margery inherited 'all the land, tenements, inheritable property and castle of Webbel' and following the death of her husband, John de Verdon, in 1274 the

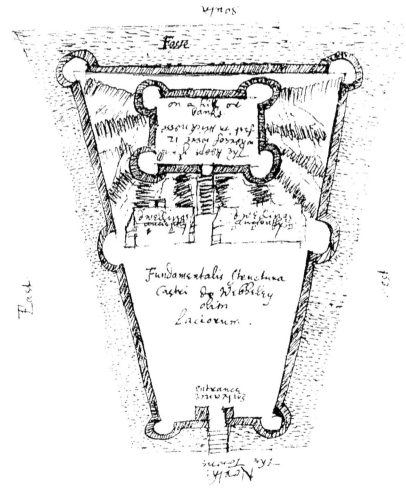

Figure 1. Plan of the castle by Silas Taylor (1655)

2. PRO, Calendar 1225-1232:305

inheritance passed to his son Theobald.[3] No information is given about the castle and no other informative references to it have been found for the 13th century.

Theobald de Vernon died in 1309. His younger son, also Theobald, inherited but died just seven years after his father in 1316 and the castle and manor of Weobley went to his daughter Margery and her first husband, William le Blount.

In 1327 and 1328 it was claimed that the castle was of no value, being in ruins. Presumably someone was suspicious about the state and valuation as a memorandum of 1332 says that the castle was valued below its worth.[4] In March of that year it was ordered 'to cause William le Blount and Margery his wife to have seisin [possession] of the castle of Webbeleye, in the county of Hereford of the value of around £81 0s'.[5] There is also mention of a chaplain of the castle at this time (Phillot 1888). Sadly the memorandum is in very poor condition, as it contains what may be the only information about the two 'dwellings' shown on Silas Taylor's 1655 sketch, as it records 'a valuation ... of the houses in the castle 20/-'.[6]

Following William's death in 1337, the castle and manor were granted to Margery and her heirs. The following year she made a grant for life of the castle to John le Blount.[7] This could well have been the brother of her late husband, referred to in the previous document as his next heir. At some time after the death of William le Blount, Margery married one Marcus Husee; this seems to be all that is known of him and neither the date of their marriage or that of his death are recorded.

In 1356 Margery married for the third time and her new husband John de Crophull took steps to ensure his rights in her property. The Calendar of Patent Rolls 1354-58 records that the king granted that 'John de Crophill, "chivaler" who has taken the same Margery to wife may retain the premises to them and the heirs of Margery'.

In the following year, one John Ailmond was pardoned for 'the breaking of his prison in the castle of Webbeleye wherein he was detained on an indictment of felony and of consequent outlawry'.[8] We have no way of knowing if his escape reflects of the poor physical state of the building or just lax security.

3. Calendar of Rolls 1242-47:210
4. Calendar of Inquisitions Post Mortem, Edward III:281
5. Calendar of Close Rolls 1330-33:481
6. See below, John Merbury's will
7. Calendar of Patent Rolls 1338-40:9
8. Calendar of Patent Rolls 1354-58:436

John de Crophull died in 1383 leaving his granddaughter Agnes sole heiress. She was still under age at the time of her marriage to Sir Walter Devereux but in 1386 he was able to claim livery of her lands, having made proof of her majority (Robinson 1869:132). In 1388, the castle came under the control of the Devereux family (who became Earls of Essex during the reign of Elizabeth I). Some ten years later, Walter de Shopdon (*sic*) says that he had the keeping of the manors of Weobley and Ewias during the minority of the heirs of Theobald de Verdon, for a farm fee of £81 11s 4d a year, by a patent granted in 1322. No mention is made of the castle.[9]

Weobley at this time appears to have been a thriving town with a wide diversity of occupations. It is of note that, following the establishment of the town, its prosperity or otherwise had very little to do with the occupancy of the castle. With few exceptions, the Lacys, Verdons and Devereux were far more involved with their Irish interests than those of Weobley and were for the most part quite content to let the town develop as it pleased, provided that it paid them what was due by way of tolls and rents, a situation which was to continue until the late 17th century, at which time the incentive for a tighter control was not commercial, but political (Hillaby 1967).

Although it has been claimed that Weobley Castle was attacked and destroyed by Owain Glyndwr (Barber 1998), no evidence has been found of any damage done at that time (see also Chapter 6).

Following the death of Sir Walter Devereux in 1402 Agnes married John Merbury of Lyonshall and for a period of time around 1417 the castle and manor were sub-let to others.[10] It seems clear from his will, made shortly before his death in 1437, that he was then living at the castle. In bequeathing his household goods to his daughter and son-in-law he mentions various places in his house (*hospitium*) where these are to be found including 'the king's chamber', the obvious implication being that at least one royal visit had been made to the castle,[11] and the likelihood is that this was one of the buildings shown in Silas Taylor's plan.

The third Walter Devereux is usually referred to as 'of Weobley'; he married Elizabeth Merbury, daughter of John Merbury. Unlike his grandfather who died in the battle of Pilleth and his son who was to die in Bosworth Field, he supported the wrong side at the rout of Ludford Bridge. In 1459 Humphrey, duke of Buckingham, was granted all the fines to be made by Walter

---

9. Calendar Memoranda Rolls 1326-7:No.908
10. Calendar of Patent Rolls 1416-22:88
11. Bannister, 1917:225. Agnes and John's tomb with twin effigies in alabaster can be found in the chancel of Weobley Church

Devereux late of Weobley for assisting against the king.[12] The following year the duke is also granted 'all sums pertaining to the king by reason of the recognisance moved in Chancery whereby Walter Devereux late of Webley in the county of Hereford, esquire, is bound to the king, in 500 marks for his rebellion' (*ibid.*).

A royal visit about which a little more is known, is that of the young Henry Tudor, later Henry VII. Having been taken captive by William Herbert at the age of four, he was later made Herbert's ward and spent much of his childhood at Raglan Castle. In 1469, following the death of her husband at the battle of Edgecote, Herbert's widow, Anne (née Devereux) took Henry to 'her family's home at Weobley', where he remained for several months.[13]

According to Salt, one Richard Keverne was appointed chaplain to serve the castle and demesne in 1471 (Salt 1953:17). It is Salt who also tells the following story:

> In 1483, Weobley was once more a centre of rebellion, when Henry, Duke of Buckingham, whose connection with the town was through the Ferrers family, rose against Richard III because, so he said, he wished to release the young princes in the Tower. When news arrived of their death, he supported the cause of Henry, Earl of Richmond. The rising entailed a movement into the county of Worcester, with Weobley as his base. He was, however, handicapped from the outset: Sir Thomas Vaughan of Tretower threatened his rear; the Severn was blocked by a flood; the leading men in Herefordshire would not support his venture. As he went forward, his troops melted away; his espionage system failed; the prophecies of his necromancer, Thomas Nardik, let him down and, finally, he was forced to flee, disguised as a countryman, in a frieze coat, leaving his servant Amgasse and their nurse, Mistress Olliffe, in charge of his two children, Humphrey, Lord Stafford, and my lord Henry. He himself was captured in Shropshire and taken to Salisbury for execution, while his Duchess was caught at Weobley. Mistress Olliffe, however, hid the children, first in the 'Little Parks' at Weobley and then in and about Kinnersley Castle, until she was able to smuggle them into Hereford riding pillion and disguised as girls (*ibid.* 20).

Phillot, telling the same story with less detail, but quoting from earlier chroniclers, speaks only of the 'house of Walter Devereux, Lord Ferrers' (Phillot 1888).

---

12. Calendar of Patent Rolls 1452-61:548
13. Griffiths and Thomas 1985:58, 59, 68

Late medieval and early post-medieval Weobley

The 16th century saw the decline of the castle as a political and economic centre. Lordship of the manor and ownership of the castle continued in the Devereux family throughout the century. The final reference to 'the castle and manor' is found in 1508.[14] The next reference to the castle is in the famous quotation by Leland *c*.1535. In November 1595 Robert Devereux, 2nd Earl of Essex, granted to Richard Tomkins, of Monnington, the lease for 21 years of 'the site of the castle of Weobley, with the castle ditch and the castle mill'.[15] It should be noted that the castle survey revealed evidence of the mill, in the form of a building platform, in Area D, located immediately west of the castle earthwork.

The 17th century opened on a dramatic note when in 1601 the absentee lord of the manor, Robert Devereux, was beheaded for treason. In 1603 Robert Devereux, 3rd Earl of Essex, regained his father's lands and honours. He died in 1646 without male issue and Weobley was inherited by his eldest daughter, Francis. On her death in 1674 she bequeathed her property to Thomas Thynne, husband of her granddaughter, Francis Finch (Phillot 1888).

Silas Taylor made a sketch in 1655 showing the keep and castle walls in plan form. It also shows the elevation of two 'dwellings' to the north of the keep, at the base of the motte and within the walls. As windows and even chimneys are indicated they may have been in a fair state of repair at that time. Were these the 'houses in the castle' recorded in 1332 or the house of John Merbury noted in 1435? Or could it be that the third Walter Devereux, who was apparently the first lord of the manor to take an active interest in it, had found the castle in such a state of disrepair that it was more convenient to have a new house built (plus an extra one) using the materials on hand? No answers have been found in the documents available but some information may be revealed by archaeological investigation.

The castle is mentioned twice in leases during the 17th century, in both cases as a secondary item in connection with the lease of the water mill. A lease of 1614 includes 'the site of the castle of Weobley' and various parcels of land but, apart from the mill, no buildings are mentioned.[16] It is clear that by this time the castle has become literally a site. The standing building survey undertaken as part of the project have revealed clear evidence of the stone being re-used. A large fireplace lintel, for example, was incorporated

---

14. Calendar of Inquisitions Post Mortem, Henry VII, No.440
15. Longleat Archives, NMR 1764
16. Longleat Archives, no reference

Plate 2. Massive lintel over a fireplace in No. 2 High Street
(Photo: D. James)

into No. 2 High Street (Plate 2). The second lease, dated 1660, includes, 'the castle of Weobley, the castle barn and fold thereto belonging with the pigeon house'. In this case, although the reference is to 'the castle', it is safe to assume that what was meant was the 'site of'.

The gradual decline of the castle continued throughout the 18th, 19th and 20th centuries. A brief resurgence of activity occurred during the Second World War, when a series of billet huts, an air-raid shelter and a tennis court were constructed within the inner bailey for US forces billeted in the village. This may have complicated the archaeology of the site, especially within the area covered by the ground penetrating radar survey (Chapter 4).

Although the castle today does not fulfill any municipal function, it has recently received much scholarly interest. The first comprehensive physical survey was undertaken by Roger Stirling-Brown and Sarah Speight through a measured survey in 1992 and identified the previously unknown remains of stone walls and foundations. A mass of buried masonry, possibly the remains of a fortified entrance to the keep, was located to the south-east of the earth-work. Further masonry is still present at the site of the north entrance to the castle (Stirling-Brown 1989). The Weobley Castle Project has surveyed the castle and five surrounding areas. The results are, in our opinion, spectacular and reinforce the idea that castles do not function in isolation.

Wind and Water Mills

The earthworks survey in Area D revealed a rectangular feature measuring roughly 25m x 15m lying close to the Millbrook. Its proximity to the stream and its position immediately north of the large holding reservoir suggest the earthwork is a water mill.

There is no mention of a mill in Weobley in the Domesday Book of 1086. The earliest reference to a water mill occurs in Nicholas de Verdun's IPM of 1271—'a mill worth 60s'.[17] Successive references describe it as ruinous in 1327 and of no value in the following year because of a lack of water. In 1332 two water mills are mentioned and this is amplified in a collector's account of 1477 as two each worth 53s 4d. In the 17th century there are accusations of Mr. Tomkyns withholding toll from a mill leased to him, but by the end of the century it seems no longer in use. The last lease was noted in 1690.

The date of 1271 gives Weobley the earliest documentary evidence of a mill in Herefordshire, predating those at Ledbury, Much Marcle and Norton Canon. The latest mention of a standing mill building is in 1710, when Anne Eckley, widow, released to John Birch of Garnstone all claim to a burgage and three acres in Weobley, next to a windmill belonging to Birch which would have been standing on Windmill Knapp.[18] No mill is shown on Isaac Taylor's map of 1786.

17. Calendar of Inquisitions Post Mortem, Henry III, No.767
18. HRO, L57/66

2 THE SURFACE EVIDENCE

Five areas—A, B, C, D, and E—were designated for both an earthworks and magnetic survey. Area A comprised around 0.3ha on the east side of the north approach to the castle earthworks in castle field. Flattish, slight depressions and humps suggested disturbance in modern times. Along its west side was a metalled path and, to the south, sharply defined, deep depressions indicated the layout of a ditch and a possible quarry area. Area B was an orchard of around 0.2ha west of the castle's north approach. Area C comprised 1.2ha around the north end of generally flat, open park land south of the main earthworks that is used for grazing. Area D was an elongated wedge of around 0.3ha along the west side of the south earthworks, bounded by the Millbrook on the west side. The earthworks gave way to a flat alluvium planted with widely spaced young trees, protected by metal fencing. Area E comprised around 1.7ha of pasture west of the stream in the Mill Parks field. A small but well-defined knoll at the north end gave way to the bed of a dry, westward-draining stream, now captured by a drain. Pronounced earthworks survived to the north-east of the knoll and elsewhere there were traces of shallow linear depressions and low banks. The survey area lies on Old Red Sandstone, a moderately hard sedimentary rock which is found across most of west Herefordshire.

The earthworks survey was designed to record all upstanding earthworks, irrespective of date, condition and origin, as part of a multi-disciplinary archaeological landscape analysis. The survey encompassed a total area of 10ha centred upon the well-preserved castle earthworks. A Topcon GTS 211 Total Station Survey System or electronic distance metering system (EDM)—which measures horizontal and vertical distances electronically—was used. Detail measurements were made either with the Total Station or by taped offsets. Ground survey data was plotted and annotated in the field at a scale of 1:500.

Plate 3. Survey training using an EDM (Photo: Tony Morris)

Weather and ground conditions during the survey period were generally very good, with the autumn and winter low light highlighting the very fine earthwork detail. Upstanding earthworks were recorded in Areas A, C, D and E. Area B, located to the south of The Salutation Inn and Corner House, had been heavily disturbed and contained no earthworks of archaeological significance.

What stood so proud: The castle earthworks

The well-preserved castle earthworks dominate the northern survey zone and encompass an area of approximately 1.5ha. A detailed plan of the earthworks has been produced by Stirling-Brown and Speight (1992). In plan, the castle is ovoid with a ring-work at its southernmost point and a bailey to the north. The earthworks of the bailey are best preserved along the eastern side, with the bank standing up to 6m high. Slight expansions and irregular linear features on the crest of the eastern bailey defences may be the result of stone robbing associated with removal of the curtain wall and towers. On the west the bank is absent and appears to have been deliberately removed to create a vista. The site of the north gate is marked by a causeway across the surrounding moat. The causeway is 5m wide with traces of a stone revetment on the east side. The relationship of the causeway to the moat suggests that it is a later addition to the complex and may be contemporary with the tree-lined avenue approaching the site from the north. The east terminal of the bank adjacent to the gate has a south-facing rectangular projection possibly indicating the position of part of the gatehouse. Within the bailey, there are no obvious earthworks apart from four low, rectangular platforms measuring 13m x 6m. These are the remains of Second World War Nissen huts built for US forces billeted in the village.

At the southern end of the bailey, a roughly rectangular ring-work measuring 30m x 40m is defined on the south and east by a substantial bank up to 7m high. Within this, there are two substantial rectangular depressions marking the position of substructures associated with the castle keep. A circular feature overlying the keep substructure appears, from its fresh and well-defined character, to be of recent origin. The plan of the ring-work is entirely commensurate with Silas Taylor's plan of 1655. On the west, the ring-work is open and it is highly probable that substantial damage to the earth-works has been caused by robbing of the castle fabric. South of the ring-work, the bailey defences are strengthened by the addition of a substantial counter-scarp standing up to 5m high and with an additional ditch on its southern side. The causeway across the moat at the south-west corner of the castle appears to be a later creation and not part of the original castle design.

Area A—Land to the north of the castle

Immediately to the north of the castle a small paddock contains earthworks and other landscape features reflecting different phases of land use. The area is bounded to the west by a stone wall containing much re-used masonry

Plate 4. The castle earthworks looking east (Photo: G.H. Nash)

15

possibly derived from the fabric of the castle. Adjacent to the wall, a metalled track leads to the entrance causeway of the castle and is flanked on its east side by an avenue of mature oak trees. The northern half of the area is dominated by a shallow, rectangular depression measuring 23m north-south and 25m east-west. Immediately to the east, an irregular mound comprises modern building debris, ash and cinders. The southern limit of the depression is continued to the east by a prominent scarp. 10m to the south, another east-west scarp is discernible with another, 10m to the south. The scarps are parallel and continue to the line of modern property boundaries to the east (Figure 2).

The metalled track and avenue of trees are best seen as part of a general planning of the landscape in the environs of the castle and would fit into a later 18th or 19th century context. The depression is of regular form and may indicate the position of a former pond, perhaps post-dating the regular use of the castle but pre-dating the planting of the avenue of trees, one of which grows from a point within the western scarp. The scarps are regularly spaced. They have the appearance of former property boundaries and may be the remains of burgage plots, similar to those that survive either side of Broad Street.

Figure 2. Plan of Area A showing a series of linear features which may represent the boundary lines of Medieval burgage plots

Area C—Land to the south of the castle

An area of approximately 3ha was surveyed to the south of the castle. The most prominent feature was a substantial scarp, up to 2m high, at the northern end of the field (Figure 3) and continuing south-west for at least 170m. To the west of this is a level valley floor with the appearance of a silted-up rectangular pond.

Plate 5. Area A looking north (Photo: Tony Morris)

The western edge of the feature was not located as it lay in an adjacent field now used as arable and all traces have been removed by ploughing. Across the northern section of the field is a low, spread bank. Another scarp 150m south of this, with traces of a hollow-way along its north side, is also parallel. The eastern side of the survey area is bounded by a further substantial scarp. A trapezoidal area defined

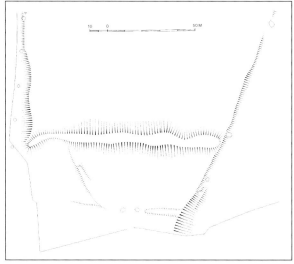

Figure 3 Area C showing a low linear bank (centre of plan) and the extent of the holding ponds (on the far right of the plan)

17

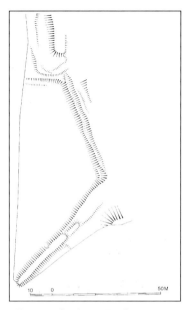

Figure 4. Area D showing a series of extensive banks and the earthworks of a possible mill (shown at the top of the plan)

by a series of scarps is clearly a former field with very slight traces of ridge-and-furrow cultivation. The northern two-thirds of the field have ridge-and-furrow aligned north-south and it seems certain that a scarp forms a denuded headland. The hollow-way is an original lane giving access to this field and a further hollow-way, aligned north-south, was recorded. This marks a boundary between a further two former fields which also contain subtle remains of ridge-and-furrow cultivation.

Area D—Land to the west of the castle

Immediately to the west of the castle, a low-lying triangular area contains earthworks associated with water management. The area is dominated by a substantial bank (Figure 4) measuring 7m wide at its base, 2.5m wide at the crest and up to 1.5m high. This is aligned north-east south-west and is visible for a distance of 60m. As it nears the western side of the castle defences, the bank becomes a single, west-facing scarp and turns through 100 degrees, continuing for a further 50m before turning west. The bank is best viewed as a dam and is part of a large, silted-up pond that continues into Area E to the west.

Area E—Land to the west of the castle

The westernmost parcel surveyed is dominated by a low hillock and contains slight, but highly significant earthworks. The eastern side of the area has two substantial banks (Figure 5) that are remnants of dams associated with a system of ponds and water management features recorded in Areas C and D. The northernmost has been truncated by landscaping of an adjacent private house and grounds, while a bank survives for a distance of 30m but has been truncated by a later field boundary. The major discovery in Area E was a series of slight, concentric scarps around the low hillock defining a sub-rectangular, bi-vallate (double bank and ditch) enclosure of approximately

*Plate 6. Volunteers surveying a large earthwork, possibly a dam
(Photo: Donald Kilgour)*

1.3ha. This is best preserved on the east, where a ditch 0.4m deep and up to 7m wide survives. Part of the ditch is overlain by a dam. In plan, the enclosure finds closest parallels with later prehistoric and early Romano-British enclosures recorded predominantly as cropmark sites elsewhere in the southern Welsh Marches (Whimster 1989). The survival of the enclosure at Weobley is of significant regional importance and may provide buried soils that will inform the environmental sequence for the area in later prehistory. No obvious entrance to the enclosure was located. South of the enclosure, a straight, linear depression indicates the course of a canalised stream.

What is going on?

The earthwork survey has provided a wealth of data on the landscape sequence of Weobley Castle and its immediate environs.

The earliest feature identified is the probable later prehistoric enclosure in Area E. The castle earthworks have provided details of the castle layout, and the location of the keep substructure suggests that substantial remains survive below medieval ground level. Beyond the castle, possible burgage plots have

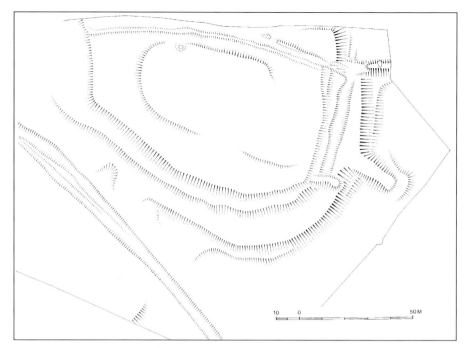

Figure 5. Area E showing a probable Iron Age enclosure and the western extent of a pond system (on the far right of the plan)

been identified to the north-east and, to the south, part of a medieval field system, probably contemporary with the castle has been recorded in detail. Traces of an extensive series of ponds and water management features have been identified west and south-west of the castle. Part of this system still requires further work to recover its full extent and function. Patches of dense scrub between Area B and Area E require further investigation and to the west of Area C, in modern arable, additional non-intrusive survey is desirable to define the extent of a large pond.

3 PROBING BENEATH THE SURFACE

To complement the earthworks survey, a sub-surface investigation was carried out using magnetic survey equipment (a Geoscan FM36 gradiometer), which detects distortions in the earth's magnetic field caused by buried ditches, hearths and walls. Technically, such features are known as 'anomalies' (Plate 7). The readings show positive and negative anomalies and these appear as a 'grayscale', the darker the reading, the more likely it is that an archaeological feature is present.

The survey aimed principally to identify features and structures contemporary with the use of the castle but lying outside the outer bailey. All five areas were surveyed using 20m-square contiguous grids. A sampling frequency of two readings per metre was applied along traverses at every metre. This rate was considered sufficient to record cut linear features, pits,

Plate 7. Using the Geoscan FM36 gradiometer (Photo: Tony Morris)

areas, including baked soil or stone, where they occurred within 0.8m of the turf and, in favourable geological conditions, to as much as twice that depth.

The readings were stored inside the instrument and then downloaded onto a computer for processing. This allowed both experts and volunteers to examine features detected by the gradiometer. Careful analysis of the grayscale has teased out many archaeological features, despite the presence of buried iron objects and features, which cause significant interference. All five areas were surveyed and the results reinforce the findings of the earthwork survey (Figure 6).

Area A

This area proved difficult to survey as iron objects and features, probably buried fencing, affected readings. Indeed, several residents remembered iron fencing in the western part of this area.

Two rows of four grids were fitted tightly between garden fences to the east and a stone wall to the west, leaving a 5m gap to the north, where further garden fencing seriously distorted the results. The plot showed the presence of iron in some form along its east, south and west sides, the

Figure 6. Raw data downloaded from the Geoscan to a computer and superimposed onto a modern Ordnance Survey sheet. Light areas represent the presence of metal

22

latter suggesting that there was an iron pipeline or buried fencing beneath a path. Particularly in the north of the survey area, many smaller metal items were detected. These, too, distorted the results of the survey.

Consequently, all interpretations are tentative. An approximately NW-SE aligned negative linear reading may be a wall or covered drain. A narrow positive linear reading extending across the middle of the survey area may be a gully or small ditch, but a trench containing a plastic or ceramic pipe is equally possible. In the south-east corner there were faint traces of a possible post-built rectilinear structure, associated with a small area that may be a refuse deposit.

Area B

Two full and three partial grids were laid out in a small orchard south of Corner House and as far as the Salutation Inn. Fallen trees obstructed the survey and showed as blank areas. A pipeline with iron components ran east-west slightly north of centre of the surveyed area and there was severe magnetic disturbance from the north to the south-east corner—probably the result of buried iron fencing or barbed wire—and in the partial grid at the south end. There were extremely tentative readings in the central and north parts of the grid and a more positive, roughly rectangular, positive linear reading in the east corner. These readings, however, remain uninterpreted. This does not mean that the area should be discounted as there may be burgage plots and possible earlier evidence of the outer bailey present.

Area C

This area, in spite of the problem of buried iron, proved to be one of the most complex, with a series of linear features, possibly ditches, intersecting other buried features.

Thirty-five full grids were laid out in an open area which included a series of holding ponds located to the west of the field. The area is bounded by wire fences on the north-east and north-west sides, alongside the latter of which was an iron pipeline. A second pipeline ran from east to west across the southern corner of the area.

There was a distinct, but still faint, positive straight linear feature of around 120m from WSW to ENE, with an even weaker intermittent negative reading along its north side. This appeared to bisect both an approximately 8m-wide positive linear feature and intermittent curvilinear features which appeared to be parts of an elongated oval. Two stronger short linear positive readings occurred towards the north corner but other negative and positive readings were very faint and displayed no coherent relationships. The one exception was a probable double-ditched feature south of the long linear feature, at its west end. It is probable that these features relate to a series of linear ditches, which may represent further medieval division of land. There is also a possibility that some of the features may relate to castle walls to the south of the inner bailey and beyond the moat.

It is notable that in a roughly 20m-wide band extending along the north side of the long linear feature all readings were weaker and less distinct than those on the south and closer to the north boundary of the area. It seems likely that the soil is deeper on the north side of the linear. The depth of the soil may relate to activity within the castle, i.e. an outer bailey area to the south of the moat.

Area D

This area proved problematic owing to the presence of extensive buried iron features, especially north and south. The five full and four partial grids lay partly over the westmost bank of the castle earthworks. In the latter, there was a weakly positive small rectilinear feature set on top of a bank projecting south-westwards from the main body of the surviving earthworks. The earthworks survey identified a similar anomaly. It is probable that a complex leat system running from the dams in Area C extend into this area. Sluices would have been placed at intervals along the leat to control the seasonal flow of water. The magnetic survey clearly showed two features cutting across this earthwork, which may represent sluices.

Area E

This area was by far the largest and most interesting. The 39 full and four partial grids were the least affected by the presence of modern iron features, such as pipelines and buried fencing. Clearly a pipeline followed the course of the stream bed and in situ modern agricultural features caused problems towards the summit of the knoll. The only other difficulties were presented by the relatively steep topography and a few widely spaced oaks.

This is the only area where the magnetic survey revealed an extensive system. Although all the readings, both positive and negative, were weak, their coherence allows a high level of confidence in the reliability of many of them, reinforced by the results of the earthworks survey. The general form is that of a hybrid or rectilinear multiple-ditched enclosure, a class well recognised in the Welsh Marches by Rowan Whimster (1989:46-49). A long right-angled positive feature appeared to be part of something larger, with two positive linear features roughly parallel with its east side. A weak double linear feature some 80m farther west was also parallel and may represent a contemporary double-ditched track leading up to the highest part of the knoll. The track disappeared beyond the point at which it was bisected by a curvilinear feature, although this seemed unlikely to be a true terminus. A slightly arcing negative feature may represent a bank nearly parallel at its east end with the south arm of the right-angled feature, but diverging from it to the west, the separation increasing from around 20m to more than 30m.

At least two sides of the rectilinear feature may comprise alignments of cut features, such as pits, rather than continuous linears. Other irregular linear features south of the knoll may derive from the changing course of the old stream.

What did the survey discover?

Following the filtration of downloaded data—from the survey equipment to a computer—each of the five areas began to reveal an interesting series of features (Figure 7). Little can be said of those identified in Area A and Area B. The anomalies identified in Area D are without doubt later than the castle earthworks, into which they appear to have been cut. In any event, all these anomalies must be treated with great caution since they are incoherent details within areas badly affected by interference from modern ironwork. Area C has produced one linear feature, which may be contemporary with at least one phase of the castle. It is probably a broad holloway which continues the line of the path through the earthworks. It appears to underlie, and hence pre-date, the intermittent negative anomaly associated with the long linear. If the latter is associated with a boundary or headland to an area of ridge-and-furrow farther south, as is suggested by the earthworks survey, that period of cultivation belongs to a later phase. The putative hollow way may have destroyed a section of the elongated oval enclosure which, if it is not illusory, must be earlier. Its form would suggest a pre- or Early Iron Age date.

The short lengths of double-ditched tracks in Area C and Area E are a form which occurs from the Bronze Age onwards. Both of these disappear at points where they meet features thought likely to pre-date the castle. By analogy with multiple-ditched enclosures from elsewhere in the Marches, the rectilinear system in Area E is likely to date to the Iron Age or Romano-British period.

In spite of the problems due to the weakness of the anomalies the survey has been very productive in the more open areas, complementing and adding to the earthworks survey. Only very few features appear to derive from the castle's impression on the wider landscape, but there are several traces and more substantial fragments of systems which probably pre-date it.

Figure 7. Filtered data showing well-defined physical features

4   GOING DEEPER

In Autumn 2002, and following the earthworks and geophysical surveys, parts of the castle were surveyed using a PulseEkko 100 ground radar system belonging to the Department of Earth Sciences at University College London. This complex piece of equipment has one major advantage over conventional geophysical equipment in that it can survey much deeper. Unfavourable weather conditions restricted the amount of work that could be done, but in the course of three days in the field it was possible to survey a block within the

Plate 8. Volunteers using the ground penetrating radar
(Photo: Donald Kilgour)

inner bailey and carry out reconnaissance work in the field west of the castle. The inner bailey has a history of minor construction since the destruction of the castle, including a role as a military camp during the Second World War, and work was concentrated in an area for which there was no record of post-Medieval development. A number of features were identified within the survey grid, although there are, of course, no indications of their age or function.

The survey lines in the fields west of the castle — in Area E — were oriented approximately north-south and must be regarded as a reconnaissance exercise only. Surveying was interrupted by rain, making the conditions unsuitable for radar work. Nevertheless, a number of features were seen on the radar sections for which there were no obvious visible explanations (Plate 8).

Ground Penetrating Radar (GPR)

GPR is a relatively recent addition to the range of geophysical techniques available for sub-surface investigation. Instrumentation relies on microwave technology developed during the Second World War. The technology relies on the reflection of electromagnetic waves. Signals are transmitted from aerials that resonate at a set of chosen frequencies. Low frequencies (i.e. long wave-lengths) require long aerials and are therefore more difficult to use, but give better penetration. Small features reflect energy back to receivers not only when the aerials are vertically above them but also when they are offset some distance on either side. In archaeological work the resulting patterns consti-tute the most common indications of human disturbance of the subsoils, in this instance the walls and structures relating to the castle. The first line in the inner bailey was surveyed at 200 MHz, but subsequent lines used the longer aerials and 100 MHz signals in an attempt to look deeper into the ground. On all lines the aerials were kept 1m apart and were moved in steps of 0.2m.

The water table is a strong reflector and will be penetrated by only a small part of any radar signal. Penetration is also affected by wet clayey soils. Conditions during the Weobley Castle survey work, in an averagely wet autumn, were thus far from ideal and the maximum penetration achieved was only around 2m.

The inner bailey survey

The initial line in the inner bailey (Line 1) crossed the site from the footpath to the eastern rampart. Two features were noted at about 1m depth and a deeper feature at about 2m. A second line (Line 2), 2m to the south, confirmed the existence of all three features. The lower (100 MHz) frequency was used on this and all subsequent lines in an attempt to obtain greater penetration, although in fact no deeper features were seen. Because of the change in frequency, the vertical scales on the plots of all lines after and including Line 2 are approximately double the scale used on Line 1, although the horizontal scales are identical (Figure 8).

Because the deepest reading, at about 8m from the start of the line, was considered to be the most interesting, subsequent work was concentrated in this area. The feature appeared weakly, and apparently at shallower depth, on Line 3, which was located parallel to and 2m to the south of Line 2, but was virtually absent on Line 5, 2m to the north of Line 1. A north-south cross line (Line 5) confirmed that the source was confined to the vicinity of Lines 1 and 2 and identified a few weak readings farther north, at depths of about 2m.

It is not possible to identify the source of the deep (or any other) reading on the basis of the radar data alone. In the case of the inner bailey survey it can only be said that the deep source is likely to be the result of human activity and that, being restricted to an area only a few metres across, it is more likely to be associated with a former construction of some sort than with

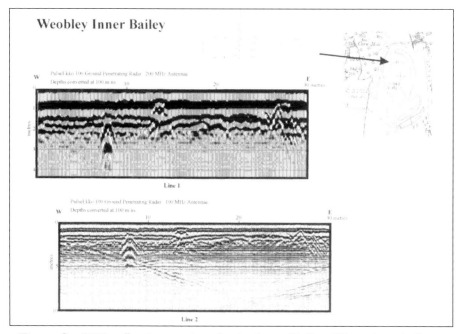

Figure 8. GPR reflection sections in the Inner Bailey. Distortions indicate the presence of a possible building

a linear feature such as a drain or water pipe. A follow-up magnetic survey of the area might provide more information, since the magnetic method is generally more successful than GPR in defining the shapes of sources in plan view.

Shallow dipping linear features prominent on the radar sections below the main signals on Lines 2 and 3 are almost certainly air wave reflections from surface features and are not thought to be archaeologically significant.

The western field survey

The field west of the inner bailey is beyond the castle site proper but, because some interesting magnetic indications were found there, reconnaissance GPR lines were surveyed, although under very poor conditions. Some readings were evident at a depth of around 2m but no surface indications of what these might be were visible and it can be concluded that a systematic GPR survey of this area would produce interesting results (figure 9).

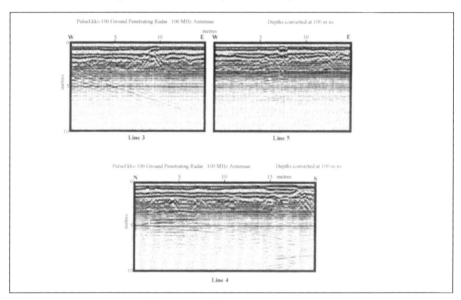

Figure 9. GPR reflection sections in Area E

5   Mapping a Landscape

As part of the project, emphasis was placed on the accurate mapping of the survey areas in relation to the castle. In addition, various aerial surveys were consulted in order to tease out more information concerning the changes to vegetation and land-use, as well as any additional information that would reinforce the results from the earthworks and geophysical surveys. The results were spectacular, especially data taken from aerial surveys undertaken in 1971 and 1983 (Figures 10 & 11).

Although this chapter deals with mapping, our story begins with the Domesday taxation survey of 1086 when Weobley was a well established settlement surrounded by about 170ha of arable land, the manor being assessed as worth a respectable 100 shillings to the Norman state. Approximately 75ha of woodland are recorded, presumably, as now, occupying the hilly ground of Burton Hill. Domesday also records a park and 'land for one plough from the assarts renders 11s 9d'. An assart is the conversion of uncultivated ground to arable and does not usually appear in Domesday assessment. That Weobley should have newly cultivated ground at this time worth over 10 per cent of its total output implies an expanding manor.

For Weobley Castle to have been militarily significant during the troubled times of Stephen and Matilda in the 1130s construction of it must have started not long after the Domesday survey. One might have expected the eminence of Windmill Knapp with its commanding views to have been chosen as a castle site within the manor in a similar strategic setting of, say, Wigmore Castle instead of the rather low position at the foot of Burton Hill.

One reason for its location may partly be due to the direct access it had to the park of Weobley and the woods and chase of Burton and Wormesley Hill. By analogy, Wigmore Castle was next to the 'Wigmore Roll' a large area of

Figure 10. An aerial survey undertaken in 1971.
This map shows the changes to vegetation, especially around the castle area
in comparison with the late 19th-century OS map

wild parkland and wood pasture at this time and used for hunting by the castle's powerful proprietors, the Mortimers. Access to the pleasures of regular hunting in an extensive area of untamed land would have been an important consideration for the siting of a castle. The evidence from a 1407 investigation into corrupt rent returns from Weobley shows Windmill Knapp to have been a long established and important area for the agriculture of the manor, as well as for the windmill or windmills.[19] A castle built here would not only have displaced this agricultural production but, to gain open access to the hunting grounds and park, the field system to the south-east would have been erased.

The early 15th century gives a little insight into the countryside which surrounded the castle. Some 31 individual enclosures, pastures, moors and strips of arable are mentioned, 26 by name, as are some of their locations relative to each other. There is a complex of tenancies among the 20 different land

19. Calendar of Close Rolls, vol.III:344. The terms of the inquiry gives a long detailed list of properties involved

Figure 11. An aerial survey undertaken in 1983. Note the oval shaped features within Area E

holders with strips of land alternating between various tenants in a way which suggests a long established farming community.

Only one of the many evocative medieval field names survives to modern times and that is the Windmill field which was still being farmed in strips by the people of Weobley in 1838 as it was 430 years earlier and quite probably 400 years earlier than that. Sadly, there is no longer a Ravensmore Meadow, Garnestone Moor, Shrewald Field, Knaven Castlefield or a Swine's Meadow, yet some of these fields will live on in what remains of the hedgerow pattern of Weobley parish.

At this time the Ley, now a farm house 1.2km west of the castle site and just 300m south-west of Windmill Knapp, was almost as significant a settlement as Weobley itself; indeed it is described as the 'town of Ley'. The four-acre field called 'Polehureu' was 'between the Ley way and the stream running to the Lord's water mill'. Just 800m south of the Ley is Fenhampton Farm whose nearby fields contain the signs of ridge-and-furrow, as well as the remains of a settlement, adding further evidence to show how much more populated was the western part of Weobley parish than now.

There are several mentions of 'moor' which may be the pre-drainage naturally marshy nature of the alluvial channel associated with the Newbridge brook which runs from the appropriately named Fenhampton to the north-east of the village, becoming the Stretford brook at the north-east corner of the parish.

The park is mentioned a few times, for example '1 acre with ditch & hedge below the moor late of Walter Brugge near the park of Thomas Bromwiche'. Apart from the name 'Knavencastelfeld' there is no other indication in the document of the presence of the castle, whose strategic significance and as a landmark seems to have declined if not become defunct. Leland in *c*.1535 describes it as 'a fayr castel of my Lord Ferrars but somewhat in decay' and it remained in sufficient repair by 1655 for Silas Taylor to sketch his well known diagram of it (Figure 1).

When most of the stone was taken is not known, but by 1872 it was a 'grass grown moat-encircled mound' according to the Rev. Charles Robinson. The first edition 25" to the mile Ordnance Survey map published in 1887 shows a few trees but not as many as now.

The proposed site of one of the mills is preserved in the field just to the west of the site in its name of 'Mill parks' and 'Castle croft' is the field to the south of the site. Apart from Windmill Fields, Windmill Knapp, none of the 1407 field names has survived.

While they do not shed much light upon the castle site itself, the changes in the landscape are most apparent. Field boundaries, orchards and trees between 1887 and 1951 show only minor differences but the change in the 20 years 1951 to 1971 is dramatic, with whole field boundary complexes removed (for example, the amalgamation of nine fields into one in the south-west corner of the frame). Also note the 1930s Land Utilisation Survey showing almost no arable, a significant fact for the history of the parish since permanent pasture and meadow is a great preserver of archaeological features on farmland. Little permanent grassland remains in Weobley parish, which is now almost 90% arable or ley. Some of the last meadows of permanent pasture at Fenhampton, which had well preserved remains of ridge-and-furrow and settlement and had been considered a possible deserted medieval village, have recently been ploughed.

The oldest and most numerous trees on the castle site and the Mill Parks field are oaks and their measurement indicates that none, even the largest, was a sapling earlier than the 19th century. Most were established by planting between 1810 and 1870. Only a few of the trees depicted on the 1887 OS map would have been big enough to merit a tree symbol and the rest have been replaced.

Measurements of the oaks have been translated into ages by reference to the one mature tree in the Mill Parks field which was pushed over at an angle in the gales of autumn 1991. When felled, its fallen butt was measured and the rings exposed by the cut photographed with a ruler. In spite of having a girth of 3.17m, only 124 rings were counted (i.e. it was planted in 1867), giving an annual ring width of 3.9mm. It can be reasonably assumed that the growing conditions of the other oaks would be similar and girth measurements can be translated into age pro rata using this one reference tree with an error of about plus or minus 10 years.

The well-known avenue of oaks that runs from the village entrance to the site to the north side of the moat range in girth from 0.420m (the second tree from the village side) to 0.288m (the last one) and reach a height of 25m. The first four oaks are quite similar in girth and range from 0.420-0.398m with an average of 0.402m, equivalent to a planting date of 1844, which is within the estimated error of 1837, the date of Queen Victoria's enthronement. The last two oaks in the avenue have much smaller but similar girths of 0.308m and 0.288m (average planting date 1887).

Two mature trees are shown on the 1887 25" to the mile OS map on the southern end of the avenue, so it is not unreasonable to assume that these were lost shortly after the survey for the map and replaced by planting 40 years or so after the first four, which would have been too small to have appeared on the map.

The oldest tree on the site has a girth of 0.487m and a planting date of 1812 assuming similar growth rates. The oldest tree on the castle site itself has an estimated planting date of 1819.

Other trees on the site are probably of semi-natural origin, being composed of native or naturalised species characteristic of the locality (Field Maple, Sycamore, Ash, Holly, Wych Elm and one Yew seedling). The woody shrub species are Hawthorn, Hazel, Elder, Blackthorn and Wild Rose. There are some ground flora species loosely associated with woodland, including Dogs Mercury, Dog Violet, Lords and Ladies, Wood Speedwell and Enchanter's Night Shade.

The grassland is moderately species rich—a rare and declining habitat—and contains a few ant hills characteristic of this habitat. A plant which may reflect the castle origin of the site is Burnet Saxifrage, which grows freely on the sides of the mound and is not usually found in local meadows where the soil is insufficiently calcareous. A detailed list of species found on the castle site has been compiled, which lists 88 plants and 19 grasses.

The two kinds of habitat studied were open grassland, including the castle mound, and the permanently damp moated area, which at the north-east of the site is in effect a long thin shaded seasonal pond. Plants there include Float Grass, Celery-leaved Buttercup and Brook Lime.

6 WHERE DID ALL THE STONE GO?

Herefordshire's rich heritage of timber-framed houses owes much to the availability of high quality, straight grained oak from managed woodlands, coupled with a long tradition of skilled carpentry. There is a recognizable regional style typified by sturdy framing and the generous use of timber, especially in the 16th and 17th centuries. There is also a distinct pattern to the layout of surviving houses as they evolved from the medieval hall, with central open hearth and in-line solar and service accommodation, to the greater comfort of the late 16th century two-storey hall with cross wings and chimney stacks.

Most of the timber-framed houses in Weobley range in date from the 15th to the 17th century. It is possible that some may belong to the 14th century, as suggested by the Royal Commission, who carried out a survey of the county's monuments in the 1930s. However, it has been established, through tree-ring dating in Wales, Herefordshire and especially in Shropshire, that no timber-framed houses earlier than about 1430 have survived within Wales itself and virtually none along the English side of the Welsh border to a depth of about 10 miles. The evidence indicates that this was due to destruction by the forces of Owain Glyndwr in the period 1400 to 1415; the firing of buildings thatched with straw must have made them easy targets. The consequence was a major programme of rebuilding that only took place after about 1425 following, presumably, economic recovery and the restoration of order. Whether this war, which spilt across the border, reaching Lyonshall, Leominster and even the suburbs of Hereford, led to damage in Weobley is not known, but it cannot be ruled out. It is, of course, possible that the presence of the castle served as a deterrent, although in the case of Lyonshall, the castle failed to protect the adjacent church, which is recorded in the Bishop's Register as having been destroyed.

The layout of the town

In Weobley, the triangular market place, laid out in front of the entrance to the outer bailey of the castle, was originally wider than today, the east side being delineated by the back lane running north from the jettied west end of 'The Elizabethan' in High Street. Market infill took place in two blocks; the buildings in the major central area lasting until the fire of 1943, leaving the east block which forms the present frontage along that side of the market area, the lane behind having fallen out of public use.

The long, burgage plots that extend back from the east and west sides of the triangular market tend to be wider towards the north of the settlement but are sub-divided at the south end, where demand for trading space has been greater.

The plots around the castle must have been restricted in depth by the need to retain the outer bailey as open space. The area south of the High Street appears on the tithe map as a single wide block, whilst in Hereford Street, a series of shallow, wide plots extends south along the west side of the road until constrained by the curve of the earthworks. It is probable that these sites represent encroachment on the castle site, although it cannot be ruled out that the rear of the plots follows the line of the outer bailey. The 1813 map and the 1849 tithe map both show that a long building once stood within the outer bailey, on the east side; this was probably a barn related to land use within the bailey, as no access is shown from Hereford Street.

The north end of Hereford Street, which was once wider than it is now, probably served as a secondary market area.

THE BUILDINGS

As part of the Weobley Castle Project it was agreed that the early houses surrounding the castle earthworks should be investigated to establish what relationship, if any, they might have with the site. The focus was on buildings along the north and east sides of the outer bailey along Market Pitch, High Street and Hereford Street. Chamberwell, a house in Chamber Walk, was also investigated. It was noted that, whilst most burgage plots in Weobley are long and narrow, those on the south side of High Street and the west side of Hereford Street are very short, clearly constrained by the presence of the castle.

Corner House

This is a two-bay, two-storey, box-framed building standing in a prominent position at the top of the central market area and on the west side of the principal entrance to the castle site. It was originally jettied on both north and east sides, although the latter has been under-built. Under the jetty there are curved brackets springing from attached shafts. The chimney stack within the west end is probably a 17th century addition. There is an extension built of stone at the back of the building in the form of a large outshot.

It is likely that this house is the surviving solar cross wing of a late medieval hall house that extended south along Castle Street. There is evidence that the wing was divided into two ground floor rooms, the parlour to the east, with the original staircase in a room to the west. The best bed chamber (solar), with its roof open to the ridge and decorated with cusped windbraces, would have been above the parlour. Access to the wing would have been from the lost hall; there would not have been a doorway directly to the street. It is suggested that the building may be mid to late 15th century in date.

Plate 9. Corner House. The site possibly represents the north-western entrance to the castle (Photo: G.H. Nash)

The most remarkable feature of the building is the shallow cellar, which is built using large blocks of neatly dressed, good quality stone. It lies beneath the entire wing but does not follow its exact dimensions, as if the cellar was made for a different building. Indications that this indeed is the case can be found in the north side where there are two wide, blocked doorways with rebates cut in the stone. On this side and in the east wall there are small, blocked window openings with splayed reveals. These and other details indicate that the cellar must once have been the lower part of a quite different building on the site and that the ground level outside was once lower by more than 1m.

Market Pitch Cottage
Adjoining the west side of Corner House is Market Pitch Cottage with its gable facing the street. This is the single remaining bay of a two-bay, two-storey, box-framed cross wing, possibly of 15th century date. It was jettied on the street front but has now been underbuilt. The present framing on the front

Plate 10. Market Pitch Cottage looking south-west (Photo: G.H. Nash)

40

elevation is misleading as it has been reconstructed to match the framing of Corner House, although the gable truss and angled braces below the tie beam are original features. The fine barge boards are noteworthy. Evidence in the frame indicates that there was no doorway on the street elevation and that windows took up the full width of the frontage.

Like Corner House, this was probably the upper (solar) cross wing of a medieval hall house but here the hall and service accommodation may have stood to the west, partly on the site of the present small building between the cross-wing and the Salutation Inn. Although only one bay of the cross wing survives it was a building of some quality, with an arch-braced collar truss over the centre of an upper chamber that would have been open to the ridge. The timbers show traces of red ochre decoration. Access to the cross wing was on the ground floor through an ogee headed doorway from the hall.

The present low building on the western side is of later construction, made from reused timber, and it is unlikely that the site it stands on would have been big enough for a hall, let alone service provision.

The Salutation Inn

This consists of a number of buildings of different dates. The earliest is perhaps the two-storey wing behind the gable on the east side, although most of the timber frame is hidden. It has barge boards from one of the market place buildings destroyed by fire in 1943. Although unlikely, it is possible that this is a cross wing related to Market Pitch Cottage, although, as mentioned above, a hall standing between the two would hardly be large enough.

The two-storey range parallel to the road on the west side was built in the 17th century and is now linked to the east wing by 18th and 19th century infill.

The curious feature of the above group of buildings is the angle change of the roadway which could indicate that, at some time prior to the 17th century, there was a realignment of the route out of the south-west corner of the market place.

Nos. 1 & 2 High Street

This is a two-storey, four-bay, box-framed range laid out parallel to the street. It was jettied along the north front but has been underbuilt in brick. The west gable end has been rebuilt in brick and much of the rear elevation has been replaced by stone.

It possibly originally formed a single dwelling but was sub-divided, probably in the 17th century, to make two separate tenements. The frame and roof structure is heavily built, the jetty joists being particularly wide (about 0.3m) with now-lost jetty brackets under alternate ones. No. 2, to the east, has been enlarged by the addition of a single-storey bay to the rear, subsequently enlarged to two-storey, above a low cellar that, in an earlier phase, served as a kitchen. A large chimney stack has been built between the front and rear bays with massive dressed stone lintels over the two ground-floor fireplaces. The one on the north side is 2.2m wide and 0.79m deep with stepped sides, whilst that on the south, in what is now the cellar, is 2.75m long.

The Royal Commission sets the date of this building as 17th century but there is reason to believe that it is more likely to be late 15th or early 16th century. It may originally have had one or two shop fronts beneath the jetty, similar to those in the nearby range along the east side of the market place.

No. 3 High Street
An early 18th century, two-storey, double-fronted brick house with a 19th-century shop front, the building has a spacious loft that has been created by

Plate 11. Nos. 1 & 2 High Street (Photo: G.H. Nash)

lowering the first-floor ceilings by about 0.75m and cutting the tie-beams to create access through the roof trusses. An opening on the east side led down to the first floor of the adjacent brick barn, providing additional storage space for business use.

Parts of the roof of the house have been constructed with re-used medieval timbers, showing evidence for a mullioned window and a plank-and-muntin screen, which could have come from an earlier building on the site.

The cellar of the house also has re-used material in the form of dressed stone for the walls and splayed stone reveals for the window apertures on the north side. However, the stone may have come from elsewhere rather than being evidence for an earlier building on the site.

The barn to the east is 18th century and has been referred to by the Royal Commission as a threshing barn although the site would make it unsuitable for such a use. It is more likely that it was a warehouse, as it has a heavily beamed, load-bearing first floor that appears to be contemporary with the walls.

Plate 12. No. 3 High Street looking south-west (Photo: G.H. Nash)

43

Nos. 4, 5 and 6 High Street

Reference to early maps of Weobley indicates that Nos. 4 and 5 High Street were built between 1813 and 1844 and that No. 6 was built between 1844 and 1885, effectively reducing the width of Hereford Street. The plot on which these three houses stand appears to have been open in 1813, although there may well have been structures on the site in an earlier period.

The Old Grammar School

This is a single-storey, box-framed building with attic rooms lit by two dormers. It has been regarded as early 17th century in date but the form of the carpenters' assembly marks, coupled with the close studding on both front and end elevations, may indicate that it was built in the mid-16th century. The porch has turned balusters and decorative carvings of the mid-17th century so it may be a later addition made when an existing building was converted following the endowment of the school by Crowther in 1653. The building is now set back from the highway which originally was wider at this point.

Castle House and Castle End

This house does not feature in the Royal Commission survey of the 1930s but the roof is reasonably early as it contains a good king-post truss, which is a

Plate 13. The Old Grammar School (Photo: G.H. Nash)

44

northern feature rarely found in this area until late in the 17th century. The middle purlin has nine, 8" (0.18m) pegs, protruding at right angles, that may have been used to take the warp threads for a loom.

Chamberwell

This timber-framed house is mentioned in a lease of 1573 and a will of 1598 but it seems to have had some major alterations in about 1700. There is evidence of a first-floor room with a medieval roof. In the garden of this house are worked stones that may have come from the castle site.

Getting some answers

With regard to the buildings around the castle site, this project raises more questions than it answers.

Corner House, the solar wing of a hall house that stood along the west side of the entrance to the castle, opens up the possibility that others may have flanked this vanished road, which is probably the 'le Castelstrete' mentioned in 14th-century documents. The maps of 1813 and 1849 do show another, separate building, behind Corner House and laid parallel to this lost street.

The jettied Corner House on one side of the castle access suggests that we could be looking on the other side for a similar corner jetty, now underbuilt, on the bricked-up west gable end of No. 1 High Street.

The precise dating of both these buildings would provide information about the status of the access in particular years.

The exact line of the boundary of the outer bailey is still problematic. What can be said with some confidence is that none of the standing buildings shows signs of the characteristic distortion, due to subsidence, that can take place in a frame built over an infilled ditch.

The cellar of Corner House, with its dressed stone walls, doorways and window openings, indicates not only that the ground level must once have been considerably lower but also that an earlier building with an undercroft appears to have stood on the site. A precise date for the present building would at least determine when the undercroft became a cellar.

The cellar under No. 3 High Street may possibly relate to an earlier building on the site, or it could be re-used stone. What is clear is that much of the material matches the stone in the Corner House cellar.

It is hard to believe that the impressive fireplace lintels in No. 2 High Street came from anywhere other than the castle and a closer study of the

Plate 14. Possible undercroft at Corner House. Elevation showing blocked-in window (Photo: D. James)

dating of both primary and secondary structures in the house could reveal more about when the castle was dismantled.

It is certain that, as the castle site fell out of use, it would have been used as a quarry, possibly over an extended period, and one would expect other houses in the town to contain identifiable stonework. There may also be re-used timber from the same source built into the Weobley houses or even, just possibly, complete structures that have been moved.

A far more detailed analysis of the houses of Weobley and a selective tree-ring dating programme would reveal much about the sequence of building within the town, all of which would help to illuminate the rise and fall of the castle site.

7   THE STORY SO FAR

The aim of the project was to reconstruct the landscape around the castle: after all, a castle is not a castle without the infrastructure to support it. It was clear from a casual walkover involving members of the history society that there were significant earthworks surrounding the castle, in particular to the south and west. Five survey areas around the castle or inner bailey (Areas A - E) were selected, each of which had a physical boundary (i.e. walls, hedges and a stream) and related to an identifiable component of the castle plan; for example, Areas A and B represented the eastern and western extent of the outer bailey. The results of the two surveys have now been processed and some interesting features have come to light.

Area A—The surveys helped establish an historical sequence of activity in this area. The outer bailey of the castle, shown by the line of the street plan (i.e. Hereford Street and High Street), dates to the late 12th or early 13th century. When the bailey fell out of use, the burgage plots visible today as a series of *c.*14th- / 15th-century earthworks running east-west, were established. Around the area of the moat are a series of linear marks that give a clue to the next phase of activity. The burgage plots were abandoned when the area became arable land, as indicated by faint 16th/17th century ridge-and-furrow cultivation marks. When the land finally became fallow, probably during the late 18th / early 19th century, a pond was created in a natural hollow in the north of the area (Plate 15).

The geophysical survey indicated an iron pipeline beneath a path running between the village and the inner bailey of the castle. A possible gully or small ditch ran across the middle of the survey, although a pipe trench is equally possible. In the south-eastern corner were faint traces of a possible post-built rectilinear structure with an associated small midden, or rubbish dump.

Plate 15. Volunteers surveying the pond (Photo: Tony Morris)

Area B—This area was initially divided into two. The southern area was not surveyed due to thick vegetation. The results from the northern area were inconclusive. The presence of iron objects or features corrupted much of the geophysical data in this area.

Area C—The earthworks survey revealed the fish ponds and associated sluice and pond system. The fish pond earthworks were extensive and ran along the western edge of the field, possibly as far as the southern boundary, towards Garnstone Park (Plate 16). An ephemeral earthwork lying south of the moat may represent the line of an outer bailey or enclosure associated with the southern part of the castle. Also found was a series of shallow ridge-and-furrow marks oriented north-south. These are probably of post-medieval origin. The geophysical results showed a series of linear ditches and a possible building. Metal piping and fencing, however, distorted many of the readings.

Area D—Lying immediately west of the castle was an area enclosed by a series of large linear banks, apparently representing a section of the dam (Plate 18). To the south, a large bank oriented east-west appeared to run across into Area E. This feature would have held back water from the fish pond closest to the castle. At the eastern end, this feature merged with another linear earthwork which delineated the eastern extent of the dam. A shallow linear

*Plate 16. Ephemeral features which represent a series of reservoirs
(Photo: G.H. Nash)*

Plate 17. Additional volunteers in Area C! (Photo: Tony Morris)

*Plate 18. Area D—extensive linear banks representing a dam
(Photo: G.H. Nash)*

depression, possibly a leat, cut into the western outer defences of the castle. The depression possibly represents an infilled leat system that can be traced in Area C. Leats, sluices and dams are features commonly associated with the sophisticated system of fish ponds characteristic of medieval castles and abbeys. To the north of the area was a rectangular earthwork which may represent a building, possibly the remains of a mill or (fish) drying house. The features in this area are probably Medieval.

The geophysics failed to yield conclusive results, owing mainly to the presence of buried wire fencing. However, there were some unclear readings, especially around the area of the rectangular earthworks in the northern part of the area. This earthwork may represent a building platform, possibly a mill or drying house (described above).

Area E—The earthworks survey revealed a series of ephemeral features which relate to the pond system. These are located close the present water course. Both surveys indicated a series of linear features, probably representing banks and ditches. These features follow the contour of the hill and may extend northwards into the village (Plate 19).

Plate 19. Area E looking south. Photograph taken from the knoll
(Photo: G.H. Nash)

The geophysical survey covered approximately 75% of the field and confirmed that this was, by far, the most important area. A number of readings suggested a substantial rectangular enclosure apparently bounded by at least two sets of banks and ditches. On top of the small hillock, evidence of a rectangular building with several buildings running north towards the village were identified. Three possible interpretations of these features are being considered. They may represent an early Medieval castle, an Iron Age enclosure or, given the presence of Roman coins in the neighbouring fields, a structure of Roman or Romano-British date.

The aim of the standing building survey was to locate any possible masonry—dressed or otherwise—within the buildings that delineate the outer-bailey of the castle. The survey did indeed identify substantial castle remains, including a massive fireplace lintel and, in Corner House, a possible guardroom.

Two groups were charged with recording the buildings along the southern frontage of High Street and the western side of Hereford Street. Chamberwell Cottage was included in the survey partly on the grounds of age but, more importantly, because it has earthworks to the rear.

The buildings along Hereford Street vary in date. Probably the most notable is the Old Grammar School, which the RCHME (1934) dates to the early 17th century but which the survey findings suggest may be mid 16th century. Opposite Market Pitch and located on the eastern side of the approach to the castle are No. 1 and No. 2 High Street. Perhaps originally a single dwelling, this building forms two tenements which are partly timber-framed and date from the 17th century. No. 2 High Street has a jetty obscured by a Georgian facade. Standing on the western side of the approach to the castle is Corner House, a late Medieval, two-storey timber-framed building with an 18th-century rear extension and a unique cellar. All four internal elevations of the cellar are constructed of finely squared sandstone blocks typical, it may be argued, of castle architecture. The internal south-facing wall has evidence of a blocked doorway and two blocked windows indicating that the ground level in High Street along the southern frontages was once much lower. This is the first direct evidence of a structure relating to the castle, the cellar being the ground floor of a gatehouse or guardroom. This further supports the argument that the line of the outer bailey extends along the High Street and Hereford Street frontage.

The field surveys and the ground penetrating radar investigations, the map digitisation and the standing building recording all suggest that the influence of the castle extended much farther than the limits of the earthworks. This inter-disciplinary approach has shown that a complex social, political and economic infrastructure existed during the active life of the castle. Its demise is also of importance and may hold the key to explaining why castles within the Marches and elsewhere fell out of use from the 16th century.

8   W<small>HAT NEXT</small>?

The first phase of the project has confirmed that, far from standing in isolation, Weobley Castle functioned as part of a wider social and economic landscape. Investigating beyond the limits of the castle mound, the field surveys have identified evidence of fish ponds, an associated leat and pond system and a possible mill site, all of which would have been essential to the viability of the castle. Traces of a much earlier landscape immediately to the west and evidence of land use following the castle's demise in the 16th century have also been revealed.

The standing building survey focused on the Medieval and Post-Medieval buildings in Chamber Walk, Hereford Street and High Street (Market Pitch) and revealed significant evidence that the castle was plundered for building stone following its demise. Corner House has evidence of an undercroft that may actually be the remains of a guardroom forming part of a gatehouse contemporary with the use of the castle. It is hoped that a more detailed survey of the houses along Hereford Street and High Street will be undertaken and that this will include the use of dendrochronology. This should precisely date the construction phases of certain buildings, thereby establishing a chronology for the demise of the outer bailey and the urbanisation of the town.

These results, made official in 2003, have posed some interesting questions that can be partly answered by excavation and further detailed analysis of the buildings surrounding the castle area. It is hoped that a number of evaluation trenches will be opened in areas indicated by the results of the earthworks and geophysical surveys. Of particular interest are the earthworks in Area E, which may represent an Iron Age enclosure. The excavation of an earthwork in Area D, which may be the foundations of a Medieval mill, is also planned. The earthworks immediately north of this site and extending south towards Garnstone Park probably represent a series of ponds with a complex leat system. A series of small trial trenches should be sufficient to confirm this.

Finally, the hope is to excavate within the bounds of the castle, provided English Heritage is prepared to grant Scheduled Ancient Monument consent. The project organisers will also need to liaise with Herefordshire Archaeology, the local archaeological monitoring authority, regarding any such plans. If consent is given, trenches will be opened in the northern and western areas of the castle site in order to ascertain the extent of the walls and to establish a relationship between the inner bailey of the castle and the main holding pond in Area D. Further intrusive investigation will take place within the central area of the inner bailey, based on the results of the ground pene-trating radar survey, which identified a rectangular structure that may be one of the buildings indicated on Silas Taylor's 1655 plan.

Phase 2 of the Weobley Castle Project will address many of the questions raised by the initial investigations. One thing that can be said already, however, is that the traditional view of the castle requires reassessment.

BIBLIOGRAPHY

Bannister, A.T. 1917. *Registrum Thome Spofford*, Cantilupe Society.

Barber, C. 1998. *In Search of Owain Glyndwr*, Blorenge Books.

Beresford, M. 1988. *New Towns of the Middle Ages*, Alan Sutton.

Beresford, M. & Finbury, H. 1973. *English Medieval Boroughs: a handlist*, David & Charles.

Botsum, R. & C., Reeves, N. 1973. *The Thomas Blount Manuscript History of Herefordshire.*

Children, G.C. & Nash, G.H. 1994. *The Prehistoric Sites of Herefordshire.* Logaston Press. Monuments in the Landscape Vol. 1.

Coplestone-Crow, B. 1989. *Herefordshire Place Names*, (BAR British Series 214).

Duncumb, J. 1804. *Collections towards the History and Antiquities of the County of Hereford*, Vol. I.

Fenwick, C. C. 1997. *The Poll Taxes of 1377, 1379 and 1381*, pt. I, Oxford University Press.

Galbraith, V. H. & Tait, J. 1950. *Herefordshire Domesday*, Pipe Rolls Soc.

Griffiths, R.A. & Thomas, R.S. 1985. *The Making of the Tudor Dynasty.*

Hillaby, J. 1967. 'Parliamentary Borough of Weobley 1628-1708', *TWFNC.*

Hillaby J. 'Hereford Gold', *TWFNC*, 1984 & 1985

Hodges, G. 1995. *Owain Glyn Dwr*, Logaston Press.

Hopkinson, C. 1985. *Herefordshire Under Arms*, Bromyard & District Local Hist. Soc.

Noble, F. 1964. 'Medieval Boroughs of West Herefordshire', *TWFNC.*

Palmer, R. 1984. *Danebury: An Iron Age Hillfort in Hampshire. An aerial photographic interpretation of its environs.* London: RCHME.

Phillot, H.W. 1888. 'Weobley', *TWNFC* (1888), 249-53.

Ray, K. 2001. *Medieval Towns in Herefordshire: a management review*, Herefordshire Archaeology Report No. 20.

RCHM, 1934. *Inventory of the Historical Monuments in Herefordshire, North West*, Vol. III.

Rees, W. 1967. *South Wales and the March 1284 - 1415*, Cedric Chivers.

Robinson, C.J. 1869. *Castles of Herefordshire and their Lords*.

Robinson, C.J. 1872. *Mansions and Manors of Herefordshire*.

Salt, A.E.W. 1953. *The Borough and Honour of Weobley*, Thurston.

Shoesmith, R. 1996. *Castles & Moated Sites of Herefordshire*, Logaston Press. Monuments in the Landscape Vol. ADD.

Sherlock, H. & Pikes, P. J. 2001. *Parkfields, Weobley, Herefordshire: A report of an archaeological evaluation*. Report No. AA/00/19.

Speight, S. 1993. 'Family, Faith and Fortification: Yorkshire 1066-1250'. University of Nottingham (unpublished thesis)

Stirling-Brown, 1989. 'Herefordshire Castles: A list of classified sites'. (Privately circulated typescript)

Thorn, F. & Thorn, C. (eds.) 1983. *Domesday Book Herefordshire*, Phillimore.

Tonkin, M. 2000. 'Windmills in Herefordshire', in *A Herefordshire Miscellany*, Lapridge.

Toulmin Smith, L. (ed.) 1910. *Itinerary of John Leland*, George Bell.

Victoria County History, *Herefordshire*, Constable, 1908.

Whimster, R. 1989. *The Emerging Past*, London: RCHME.